First pu

©]

ISBN:
978-1-78972-282-6

Published by Independent Publishing Network

www.davyedge.wordpress.com

Printed by Relay Print, Wallasey, UK

This book is dedicated to my cousin,
Hannah May Clare,
for her love, support, patience, practicality,
and her logical mind.
Without her, artistic chaos and random
disorganisation would be my lot.

PREFACE

If I have a mission statement
when I fill my pen with ink,
it is to make you, dear reader,
laugh, or cry, or think.
There are no other motives
behind my choice of words.
Anything that's not worth saying,
well, I'll leave that to the birds.
My subject is the Human Condition,
and all that's contained therein.
I'm not concerned with judgement
on what is or what isn't sin.
I search the meaning of melancholy,
hidden joys to find.
I explore the depths of the humble soul,
and seek out the beautiful mind.

For on that level of consciousness,
I pray our minds will meet,
beyond the mechanics of daily life,
to where spirit is complete.
Above the mountain of broken dreams,
and valley of despair,
there is a place called Peace;
read on,
and I will meet you there...

FOREWORD

I was pleased to be one of the people who encouraged Davy to publish his first book of poetry, and I am delighted to write this foreword to his second book. Many times on my radio show, Davy shared  his gift of understanding and communication to share his battle with Bipolar Disorder with my listeners, frankly and honestly, and I'm sure many listeners benefitted from his words. Davy has poems for everyone and for every thing, and his gift is that everyone can understand them. There's no deep message . . . no hidden meaning . . . just words that are written with a pen dipped in emotion, passion, understanding, and love . . . I hope his ink never runs out.

Billy Butler
July 2019

CONTENTS

A Broken Heart	40
A Literary Life	8
A Man for All Seasons	9
A Moment in our Hands	50
A Musical Instrument	71
A Penny for your Thoughts	68
Alcohol	41
All That Stuff	20
At Peace	10
Be Still	11
Bleed	21
Brief Encounter	22 and 23
Carpe Noctem	16 and 17
Chameleon	15
Change	18 and 19
Coat	12
Conundrum	13
Dear Teenagers	52 and 53
Evensong	65
Excess	14
Exeunt Omnes	24
Flow Gently, Sweet Mersey	26
From the Heart	25
Getting There	29
Ghost at the Table	28
Gifts	30
Gossips	44
Happy Hour	38 and 39
In Disguise	67
It Will Get Easier	70
La Cuenta de la Vida	2
Life is Good	66
Listen	64
Live Fiercely	62
Lost	27

CONTENTS

Love Mantra 51
Love Yourself .... 56 and 57
Naked 33
Nicotine 31
Old Soul 63
On the Wearing of Tweed 32
Once 54
One 34
Open 61
Orphan 37
Paradise, Almost 36
Perhaps 35
Robin 3
Simplicity 60
Spark .... 74 and 75
Speak 58
Stars 77
The Absence of You 59
The Art of Calm 55
The Bard of my Backyard 76
The Child Within 73
The Comfort Zone 6
The Darkling Dusk 1
The Dentist .... 78 and 79
The Doubting Ones .... 42 and 43
The Joys of Nature .... 4 and 5
The Greater Shame .... 80 and 81
The Oldest Man in Oldham .... 46 and 47
The Sparkly Dust 83
This Road 82
Troubadour 7
Trudging Through Treacle 72
Waiting Room .... 48 and 49
Wisdom 69
Worth 45

The Darkling Dusk

O! My darling!
The darkling dusk
falls over eventide.
Heavy is the scent of musk,
as sun's brief hours subside.
Apollo and Calliope dance,
to kiss away the day.
They greet the night with sweet romance,
and, in those moments, play.
I breathe in words, as they drop from their lips,
and drift into my soul.
O, that I may their mouthpiece be!
May I fulfill that role!
For the humble poet
is privy to their play;
translator of their passion;
interpreter of their say.
So may I, with steady hand,
transcribe each sacred thought.
Diamonds drip like dewdrops,
and in my net are caught!
O, that I may overhear
each uttered word and rhyme;
and from that tryst a picture paint,
of love at evening time.

La Cuenta de la Vida (The Bill of Life)

The Bill of Life must surely be paid
by those who've been present on the mad parade.
Nothing ever comes for free,
in the creation of our destiny.
Therefore, we must pay the price,
for every habit, and every vice.
For what we sow, so shall we reap;
so, on nights when pain interrupts your sleep,
count your blessings, rather than sheep!
For Life is meant to be Lived to the full;
any other existence would be dull!
The physical shell may hurt like hell,
but, oh, the stories you can tell!
So never complain, if you've given it all,
for once upon a time, you had a ball!
Accept the aches and pains it's brought,
and keep yourself in positive thought!
Life should be lived with a capital 'L'!
Be happy to pay for dining well!

Robin

There's a robin in my garden;
he turns up every day.
His breast is as red as fire,
and he comes as if to say:
"I am watching over you,
whether you like it or not.
I am the spirit of Spring's new hope;
the ghost which time forgot.
I come to dry the moistened eye,
and make the weary strong.
My presence lifts the very heart
of those who hear my song.
I am here, through hail and rain;
through sunshine, and through snow.
I bring to you my beauty,
to set your heart aglow.
So have no fear of tomorrow;
for sufficient is the day.
The past is gone forever,
and, like old leaves, blown away.
I bring you the present moment,
to do with as you please.
Find content within yourself,
and your current torment, ease!"

The Joys of Nature

The heavy tweeds of winter
are in the wardrobe, hung.
Leaves are growing upon the trees;
'tis spring, and birds have sung!
The lawn requires its first mow;
buddleia needs cutting back.
The old stone wall, not five feet tall,
has a nest in every crack.
O! The joys of Nature,
as Life begins to bloom!
Gone the dark, damp evenings;
gone, the sense of gloom!
The bee is being industrious,
pollinating away;
every living organism
seems to have something to say.
O! The joys of Nature,
as she wears her brand new clothes!
I take in all her beauty;
on the air, the fragrant rose.
From the pond comes the sound of frogs,
croaking in monotone.
With all the wonderful wildlife here,
it's hard to feel alone!
The tranquility of a garden
on a day in early spring...

There's nowhere else in all the world,
which such delight could bring!
O! The joys of Nature!
I treasure in her gift!
I take my pen and paper,
and set my mind adrift...

The Comfort Zone

Once,
I lived in the comfort zone,
and didn't go outside.
I drew the curtains,
so no-one could see;
'twas a safe and secure place to hide.
I lit my candles, and my fire,
and kept my world unseen.
But one cannot stay in the comfort zone,
and realise one's dream!
If goals are to be attained at all,
we have to leave the womb;
and seek out opportunity,
beyond our smothering tomb.
The comfort zone is a marvellous place,
to think, to write, to heal;
but there comes a time in everyone's Life
for passion, and for zeal!
For if we cloister ourselves away,
and never see the Light,
we'll never know the wonder
of watching ideas ignite!
So! Leave that vacuous hinterland,
and set your sails anew!
Far away from your comfort zone,
you'll find the magic in you!

Troubadour

It is with grace, I accept my lot;
a wandering troubadour, I.
I perform my lyrical ballads,
and bring a tear to the eye.
The wage is only material,
though sustenance it brings.
It is a far more permanent tryst,
which makes the heart want to sing.
It is the joy of music,
and creation of the same,
which brings the voice to liberty;
no bars, no ropes, no chains.
It is the hands of the audience,
which bring about good cheer;
the sound of honest clapping
being pleasant to the ear.
And should the lyric make you think,
then my words have been well-heard.
I wish you Love, and Light, and Peace,
now that my tune is air'd.
I am a wandering troubadour,
for 'tis my worldly lot.
Remember me in your heart of hearts,
lest I should be forgot.

A Literary Life

Forsaking love and passion,
I pursue my art alone,
walled up in my tower,
of cement, and of stone.
Gone, the stomach butterflies;
gone, the broken heart.
I choose to live a literary life;
no tears to sting and smart.
As long as I have pen in hand,
and paper, at my whim,
I find contentment in solitude,
away from the bustle and din.
In this game of solitaire,
my mistress is the Muse.
She doesn't conform to the worldly norm,
and does not my heart abuse!
She is my morning, noon, and night;
my waking thought, my Inner Light.
Live to create!
Create to Live!
And to all else, no credence give!

A Man for All Seasons

Thirty-eight winters have passed,
since last I looked upon his face.
I speak with him in casual tones,
for our bond was more than blood alone.
Finest friend of my childhood days;
shaper of my errant ways;
beautiful of soul, and mind;
more of a gentleman you'd never find.
Words of wisdom he'd freely impart;
(I have them saved in my head, and my heart).
Gentle in manner, kind in thought;
strong in values, fearing naught.
Happy, I could ever be,
if I were half the man as he.

At Peace

I am at peace,
though my heart be heavy
with the loss
of those I have loved.
I have found stillness
through grief;
and patience,
through long hours
spent in silence,
listening to the rain.
I have taken comfort
from small victories,
and strength from adversity.
My spirit is uplifted,
and I am at peace.

Be Still

Be still.
The night breathes silence,
at the death of long day.
So many thoughts
have come, gone,
and passed away.
Nothing now to feed upon;
nothing left to say.
Be still.
Be still,
at the death of long day.

Coat

I have a coat which I once wore.
It used to hang behind the door,
ready for walks in the rain, and such.
I don't wear it now, as I don't go out much.
It hangs above an old pair of boots,
at the back of the wardrobe, behind the suits.
I can't bring myself to throw it away,
in case it rains again, someday.

Conundrum

Some things are never meant to last,
and some, to never be.
Accepting the great conundrum,
is what will set us free.
We pine for this, we pine for that;
we long for heart's desire.
We search for love, like hungry dogs.
Instead, to Life aspire!
For love will find its own way home,
if left to its own device;
it doesn't need to be hunted down,
as cats hunt after mice.
Life should be our purpose here;
all else falls into place;
So get on with the job of Living;
to love, be no disgrace!
For it comes when good and ready,
where hearts in harmony beat.
Therefore, Live, with love for Life,
and loneliness defeat!

Excess

Whatever it is,
give me too much of it.
Let it feed my constant hunger,
and my fatal curiosity.
I want to fill my heightened senses
with everything,
until I'm sick,
and turn the colours of a dirty rainbow.
Let me bathe in freshly-fallen snow,
and dry myself on pampas grass.
Bring me bergamot, and lavender,
that I may gorge on their scent.
Let me be everything;
for nothing begets nothing;
and I am too long given to boredom.
Above all...above all...
keep your mediocre emotions,
and your disapproving looks,
for I tolerate not the mundane.
It strangles my dreams,
and smiles the smile of the crocodile.

Chameleon

The clock, again, strikes four a.m.
Memories knock
at my front door,
playing out what went before;
what was, but will be
nevermore.
Oh, my changing, changeling heart!
How you loved to dance!
Oft, have I tired with morning light,
in the heat of fine romance;
my tie askew, my clothes, unkempt,
the taker of a chance.
Now, I wind the bedroom clock,
and extinguish the candle's flame.
Try as I may, I cannot stay
the workings of my brain;
for it always has too much to say,
when the world has gone to bed,
and I am here, in solitude,
with daylight hours fled.
And in these quieter moments,
my chameleon skin is shed.

Carpe Noctem

Beyond the dark, dismembered clouds,
I saw a ray of light.
It fell upon the fertile ground,
and stayed there until night.
Ah! Night! When folk are fast asleep,
huddled up in bed,
dreaming dreams that may never be,
I live my dream instead.
For who could want a notion more,
when all the world's a rhyme?
The aching beauty of language
makes a liar of time.
Sweet melancholy sentences,
hover about my ear;
brought about by lack of me,
when day is dank and drear.
But, O, the Night! The lovely Night!
I am unfettered then!
Open fire, and candlelight,
and words to bleed from pen.
Speak to me! O! Speak to me!
You blessed angel! Speak!
Release me from the blustery day;
rain kisses on my cheek.

Beyond the dark, dismembered clouds,
the ray of light holds fast;
until the glorious night time comes,
and day, once more, is passed.

Change

"Would you like to change your mind?"
The question's often asked;
how deeply we consider it
almost an impossible task.
We cannot change how we've been born,
but we can change how we think.
Nothing is ever set in stone,
or written in indelible ink.
Too often we play the victim
to circumstances past;
we blame our situation
on how our Lives are cast.
We wallow in self-pity,
and curse our wretched bones;
we beat ourselves up, night and day,
with constant sighs and moans!
"What if this?" and "What if that?",
and "Why me? It's not fair!"
Imagine how Life would suddenly improve,
if those thoughts disappeared in thin air!
Imagine how free our heads would be
if we shrugged those illusions away,
and employed the great and subtle art
of detaching from yesterday!
There are things we cannot change,
which are out of our control.

Leave them be, and learn from them.
Learning is good for the soul.
And so I wish you a positive day;
and, if peace is hard to find,
remember, sometimes, all it takes
is a little change of mind!

All That Stuff

Sometimes, the night is not enough,
with its moonbeams and stars,
and all that stuff.
And fancy poetry! What's that for?
The wolf is howling outside the door!
And poets seem to die alone!
Virginia Woolf filled her pockets with stones.
Sylvia Plath decided on gas;
Hemmingway, also, chose to pass.
And, yet, my Light keeps burning on.
I will not be the next one gone;
for purpose is my driving force.
My sight is set on my chosen course.
There are many thoughts inside my head;
and many words, as yet, unsaid.
They wait for her who guides my hand,
though my heart will never understand
why, sometimes, the night is not enough,
with its wishful dreams,
and all that stuff.

Bleed

It is that hour of the night,
when I bleed thoughts onto the keyboard.
I could use the word 'type'
but it would be the wrong word.
Typing suggests efficiency;
like a typist in a typing pool,
ever so professional, ever so cool;
rat-a-tat; rat-a-tat;
that is where the typist's at.
But I bleed.
Slowly.
Painfully, sometimes.
Not from my fingertips,
but from my core.
I could sprinkle the paper with trifles,
and be merely an entertainer
of shallow degree,
bringing momentary thrill
with my worthless art.
But I bleed,
from every pore.
It comes seeping,
with each stretch of imagination,
until my mind stills,
and my exhausted heart
cries no more.

Brief Encounter

It was just a brief encounter;
two strangers on a train,
planning separate journeys
from the station, in the rain.
They'd both embarked at Euston,
and sat in opposite seats.
Two lonely souls, adrift in time,
which opportunity meets.
He commented on the dreary day,
as water streaked the glass.
She took her book from inside her bag,
to make the hours pass.
The train sped on until Milton Keynes,
when he asked her of her name.
She gave the information,
and asked of him the same.
By the time the train reached New Street,
they'd shared a pot of tea,
and bought some overpriced sandwiches,
from the buffet in carriage three.
They talked of family holidays,
with spouses, since passed on;
and showed each other photographs,
taken in days long gone.
As the train pulled into Lime Street,
she stood, and bade him farewell.

He seized the moment, in his stride,
for she'd more of her story to tell.
He had a golf umbrella,
which offered shelter for two.
She agreed to share its benefits,
while they waited in the taxi queue.
Just a brief encounter;
two strangers on a train,
never knowing if happiness
would ever come around again.
And so, this thought I leave with those
who are lachrymose, lonely, or lost;
never, ever, give up on Life,
no matter what the cost!

Exeunt Omnes

Macbeth saw his end when Macduff quipped
that he was, from mum's womb, untimely ripped.
Bit of a drag, that, for Macbeth,
who thought that he had conquered death.
Likewise, Laertes, on his poisoned sword,
manages to end up being gored,
while Hamlet, who may or may not have been mad,
claims revenge for his poor old dad.
Antony and Cleopatra take their own lives.
Cassius and Brutus die on their knives.
Romeo and Juliet, Ophelia too,
Othello, the Moor...and that's only a few.
What is it with characters in Shakespeare's plays?
Can they never naturally end their days?
I expectantly turn another page,
in case someone dies of mere old age...

From the Heart

I am touch'd with fire.
My soul is ablaze,
and the Universe is mine to hold.
Each tiny, breathing, living thing
speaks in colours bold,
and I am Alive.
I am open to this moment,
and its infinite possibilities;
for my mind is as keen as
the eye of the archer,
and as sharp as the arrow,
tensioned, and ready to fly.
Wherever it takes me, I will follow,
with all my being;
for what is mind without heart,
but shallow imaginings,
cast, carelessly, into nothingness.
O! That I may create my art,
only, ever, from the heart!

Flow Gently, Sweet Mersey

Flow gently, Sweet Mersey,
with your rectilinear tides.
Pilot! Bear me past the bar,
toward the Irish side.
The land of Yeats and O'Casey waits,
and the voice of Behan speaks.
In culture I'll drown, from Dublin Town,
to Mcgillicuddy's Reeks.
Treasures of the Celtic pen are mine,
to devour and digest;
diamonds of the finest cut,
e'er found in east, or west.
Music of whistle, and uillean pipes
lays softly on the air.
Though many are gone to the Stars and Stripes,
they leave their spirit there.
And in that marriage of word and song,
history is written.
Rosaleen tells her secrets, all,
to hearts, forever smitten.
Flow gently, Sweet Mersey,
with your rectilinear tides.
Carry me to the sacred ground,
over the water wide.

Lost

When love's lost in the morning,
we have to face the day.
It's hard to focus on anything,
except what's gone away.
We get that sinking feeling,
and doubt starts to attack.
All manner of troubles beset the heart,
when love's not coming back.
When love is lost at lunchtime,
it puts us off our food.
We stare at plates piled high with fare,
but we're really not in the mood.
The seemingly carefree morning,
is washed away in a trice;
hands are clammy and mouth is dry,
and they're as cold as ice.
When love's lost in the evening,
we spend the night alone;
wondering at what might have been,
had love not upped and flown.
The bed is far too empty,
and the mind too full to think.
It hurts whatever time of day
love goes on the blink.

Ghost at the Table

There is a ghost at the table,
where I was wont to sit;
a single, solitary shade am I,
without an ounce of wit.
Make you merry, gentlemen;
and, ladies, dance away.
For I will bid a fond farewell,
having no inclination to stay.
I have seen the neon lights,
illuminating the sky,
and tripped the light fantastic,
and been left, high and dry.
There is a ghost at the table,
playing a dead man's hand;
the final chips have been put down,
in strategy unplanned.
The throbbing of the music,
cannot change my mind.
I've no desire to lead the choir,
in the kingdom of the blind.
So make you merry, gentlemen;
and ladies, dance away.
For I will to my nest retreat,
and there, in comfort, play.

Getting There

"I'm getting there" I heard you say.
Well, I'm glad that I've caught you, on your way!
Where is this place you're heading for,
where total recovery lies in store?
What's wrong with where you are right now?
It's where you need to be, and how!
Life rushes along at a heady pace;
sometimes we're running like rats in a race!
In our sights is a mythical land,
where all will be revealed, and we will understand.
So! While you're 'getting there', my friend,
on the journey you perceive to have an end,
enjoy each moment as it comes your way.
Take the time to make the most of the day.
For you can be nowhere, but right here, right now!
You've arrived. You have 'got there'.
Stand up! Take a bow!

Gifts

I love the smell of new-mown grass,
light, on the spring morning air.
No man can know its treasures,
lest, in the moment, he's there.
I hear the song of the robin's call,
as it chirrups through the trees.
My ears are open to nature's sounds;
the garden is loud with bees.
Forsythia, in its glory,
sits pleasant on the eye,
up against the old stone wall,
almost five feet high.
If we stop to appreciate Life's little gifts,
our journey becomes blessed.
They bring a song to the weary heart,
and fire to the breast.
Next time you look at the speeding clock,
O, journeyman to the minute,
remember to take a moment for yourself,
to Live the Life within it!

Nicotine

Damn you, dreadful Nicotine!
You're a monkey on my back!
If only I could shake you off...
(after one more pack).
You cost a fortune, so you do.
You make my clothes smell bad.
You're going to be the end of me,
like you did for my poor old dad.
I'd like to taste my food again.
I'd like to smell the flowers,
but I've done without you once before;
it was a terrible twenty-four hours.
I wake up every brand new morn,
with quitting on my brain;
but then I make a cup of tea,
and the pattern remains the same.
I will beat you, Nicotine!
I will, indeed, one day!
You're as false a friend as alcohol.
You're a devil in your own way.
I'll kick your butt to Kingdom Come,
for I'm a warrior and a fighter.
I feel better, now that's off my chest...
I've finished.
Where's my lighter...?

On the Wearing of Tweed

I wholeheartedly encourage the wearing of tweed.
It suits a chap's most every need.
Women, too, can gain much joy,
as can every girl and boy.
Simply wearing an item of tweed,
gives a dash of panache, indeed;
and hearkens to a bygone age,
when chic, and style, were all the rage.
Modern dress isn't meant to last,
here for a moment, then, gone in a blast.
If you want something that's going to endure,
don't look to fashion for a cure!
Search no further than clothing of tweed,
from Donegal, Harris, or Austin Reed.
Houndstooth, puppytooth, and herringbone;
take your pick, and make it your own.
Wear it when casual; wear it for best;
you'll always be impeccably dressed.
Now, no longer, is tweed to be,
the material of the aristocracy.
You can pick up a bargain in the charity shop,
or go to eBay for the cream of the crop.
Either way, there is a need
to possess, at least, one piece of tweed...

Naked

Show me your naked soul.
Bare it before me.
Tell me the thoughts
which keep you from your bed,
when all the world's asleep,
and your flickering flame
struggles its spark to keep.
Speak to me with your eyes,
that I may see Truth.
For I desire to know you;
not as the world knows you -
all clothed,
and wearing your well-worn smile,
but as you know yourself -
better than you know yourself,
if you know yourself, at all.
I would tell you to love yourself;
not for anyone's sake but your own.
Understand yourself,
because learning is part of your journey.
Be kind to yourself,
because you have to live with you,
in that place where you are always
totally
naked.

One

One.
That's what I asked for.
Not two.
One.
Two is for when there are two of you;
you and another...
a significant other.
One,
is what I told them.
And yet they gave me two.
"Included in the 'bogof' deal."
Now, what am I to do?
You would have eaten the other one,
that is, if you were here.
It seems a shame to waste it,
this bargain of the year.
I could feel magnanimous,
and give the thing away;
or maybe put it in the fridge,
to eat another day.
Though innocent on the face of it,
all it did was remind me of you.
And so, I ate it as comfort food.
I'm glad, now, they gave me two...

Perhaps

Perhaps, it'll rain today.
Perhaps, it will. Perhaps, it won't.
Perhaps, I'll plan a holiday;
Perhaps. But what if I don't?
Perhaps, I'll never feel better than this,
and the rest of it is downhill.
I've come to the conclusion that all this 'perhaps'
is starting to make me ill!
Better to stay in the moment,
and take things as they come,
than waste this time wondering
how the day ahead will run.
The future is merely guesswork;
for none of us can know
what lies in store around the bend,
'til around that bend we go!
I'll content myself with the here and now,
and not put tomorrow to test.
I'll Live my Life as it happens.
Perhaps, that'd be for the best!

Paradise, Almost

Some people like the forest;
others prefer the coast.
Whatever it is that floats your boat
is Paradise, almost.
If, when you are hungry,
you dine on gypsy toast,
or hot bread, dipped in hummus;
that's Paradise, almost.
When days are filled with laughter,
and letters in the post,
containing hearts and flowers,
that's Paradise, almost.
But when the ball is over,
and you're dancing with a ghost,
you'll find you're not prepared for the hell
of Paradise, almost.

Orphan

No stories or tales, now, for this child,
to keep me safe in the uncaring wild;
no thoughts to set my mind to sleep,
or to comfort me, when I weep.
All to dust are the bestowers of my day;
there is nobody, now, my fears to allay,
on nights when the wind is higher than the moon,
and the bad things darkle in the corner of my room.
O! To see those darling faces once more!
T'would surely lift my heart, and make my spirit soar!
Yet, all is finite, save the soul,
carried around in mortal mould.
I founder, as on an angry sea.
What is to become of me?

Happy Hour

The sign outside read 'Happy Hour';
he sat at the bar in tears;
looking for the answer
in one of the pub's cold beers.
Not even the cheapness of the drinks,
nor the barmaids shapely rear
could bring a smile to his sullen face,
or distract him from his beer.
What he hoped to find in there
was anybody's guess.
What lies at the bottom of a bottle
is a sad and sorry mess.
Yet, many have trodden that road before,
and the result is always the same.
Added problems are brought to the fore
when we play the drinking game.
It comes along in friendly guise,
and brings a comforting glow;
then it opens up the stopcocks,
from which all emotions flow.
It takes away our self-respect;
our family, and friends.
It wants to have us all to itself,
so the misery never ends.

The sign outside read 'Happy Hour'
yet, the truth is a different tale.
Happiness will never be found
in spirits, wine, and ale!

A Broken Heart

Perhaps he died of a broken heart,
that no medicine could have cured.
Every day he waited,
was a day to be endured.
They never came to visit, of course;
though I'm sure they wished him well.
After all, they were family;
(not that anybody could tell).
He'd lost his wife ten years ago,
and, since, had lived alone.
Though his hands were too frail to use it,
they'd bought him a telephone...
to keep in touch with the grandkids,
who were out in the world having fun...
too busy to bother with grandad;
"He'll live, when all's said and done".
Perhaps it was in those moments,
he gave up the ghost and died.
Perhaps there were too many memories;
too many to hold inside.
Perhaps it was then that his heart gave out;
when the tide was at its low.
Perhaps, it was then that he chose to move on.
Perhaps. We will never know.

Alcohol

Alcohol – the Demon, Drink;
the false and spurious friend.
Hanger-on to Hope's desire,
and maker of our end.
How welcoming those arms have been,
inspiring conversation.
Unaware of its wicked wiles,
I yielded to temptation.
I slipped my hand into its fire,
and willingly walked along,
until my soul began to tire;
gone, my former song.
Friend, indeed! It owns my name!
I know myself no more!
It eats away at all I am,
with every glass I pour.
And yet I will deny its hold!
(in that, I deny myself.
For who would not give all, to Live
in contentment, and in health?).

The Doubting Ones

"I wouldn't do that, if I were you.
Don't you know your place?
What if everything goes wrong,
and you've omelette on your face?
Don't expose your soul to all.
You're likely to end up hurt.
At the very least, some vicious beast
will go around dishing the dirt".
Never listen to the doubting ones,
for they'll put a damper on all!
Live your Life as a freebird,
for too soon comes the pall!
Follow the whisperings of your heart,
and to yourself be true.
Don't listen to the doubting ones,
who never see things through.
Pay attention to your passions,
and give your dreams full rein.
All things can be possible,
if, dedication you'll entertain.
Don't listen to the doubting ones,
who think you should act your age.
You can feel their negativity,
as they pace about their cage!

Nothing, I'm sure, would ever get done,
if we listened to their cries!
Be young of spirit, and brave of heart!
That's what I would advise!

Gossips

Gossips are the worst of the worst;
they really get my goat.
Whenever I hear gossip,
I put on my hat and coat.
It's certain to involve somebody
who all the parties know.
Some poor soul is the subject,
when stories start to flow.
Gossips aren't sure where they heard it first,
but that never cramps their style;
as long as there are some juicy bits,
the truth can be missed by a mile.
Avoid these people at all costs,
for they're happy to dish the dirt.
It really matters not a jot,
if anyone is hurt.
Neither repeat, nor listen, to gossip,
for it belongs on the tongues of the weak,
who cannot fill the void in their lives,
and so, about others, speak.
Keep your counsel well, my friend,
for respect is thereby earned.
It is the ones with running mouths
who get their fingers burned.

Worth

On days when you wonder why you were born,
contemplate simply this...
Who did you say hello to today?
Whose cheek did you fondly kiss?
Who has benefitted from your words,
either now, or sometime gone?
Who have you been there for,
when only hope lingered on?
How often have you made that call
to a friend, who is in need?
How long have you sat on the telephone,
listening to someone's heart bleed?
Never question your reason
for being on this earth!
You are a needed soul, indeed.
Be aware of all your worth!

The Oldest Man in Oldham

The oldest man in Oldham,
was older than the hills.
He put it down to staying young
by taking vitamin pills.
He religiously ate his five a day,
and followed a healthy regime.
He kept a picture of his long-deceased wife
by his telegram from the Queen.
He didn't smoke, and liked a joke,
and was proud of his prize winning marrow.
He often told tales of days of pale ales,
and selling fruit from a barrow.
He'd enlisted in the army,
the day that war broke out.
"I chased that Mr Hitler
both here, and thereabout."
He'd lost his eye for reading,
and listened to radio plays.
He'd enjoy a biscuit, and a cup of tea,
in dreams of his salad days.
His neighbour did his shopping,
and folk often knocked at the door.
He was happy to tell he was doing well,
for a man of a hundred and four.
Alas, he passed away today.
There was no pain, nor rage.

He went to sleep and didn't wake up,
succumbing to extreme old age.
They'll lay him in the churchyard,
with his gone-before family;
and leave the world to silence,
beneath a rowan tree.

Waiting Room

In the doctor's waiting room,
all sorts of folk can be found;
waiting on treatments for ailments,
when the doctor comes back from his round.
Some are there with sniffles,
and should really be in bed;
not infecting others,
with all their germs outspread.
Coughs which are almost percussive
bellow from people's chests.
They're waiting for a stethoscope
to be put inside their vests.
The little boy, with his fluffy toy,
is playing musical chairs.
His mother is reading a magazine,
she's the recipient of angry glares.
"He's just stepped on my broken toe"
came one indignant call.
"You should keep your children under control,
if you bring them out, at all".
The receptionist (who's never been kissed)
is answering the phone.
She's dreaming of a boyfriend,
who'd love to take her home.
A delivery man (whose name is Stan)
brings boxes in on a truck.

I hope he makes it with the receptionist;
they deserve some romantic luck.
Everyone here has a little fear,
as nobody wants to be ill.
Hopefully we can be sorted out
with a powder, and a pill.
So here I sit in the waiting room,
waiting, with the rest of the sick.
It's an easy way to discover
how other people tick!

A Moment in our Hands

I held a moment in my hand;
it weighed no more than a grain of sand.
Yet, it sustained me through the day,
when other moments had slipp'd away.
Therefore, share this moment with me;
let your mind, and your heart, run wild and free.
Lose those heavy, heavy chains,
Let your spirit rise through sad remains;
and, in this moment, find your fire;
open your eyes, and lift senses higher,
for we will never pass this way again.

Love Mantra

I'd rather be with someone
who was proud
to be with me
because of who I am,
than someone
who was embarrassed
to be with me
because of who I'm not.

Dear Teenagers

Dear teenagers,
we beat you to it.
We've driven too fast in the car,
been drunk,
and smoked the odd joint.
We've trailed home at four in the morning,
wondering where we'd left our morals,
and shirked work on sunny days
to run barefoot across a sandy beach.
AND...we've managed to stay alive!
In spite of everything, we've survived!
So when you pass us on the street,
and think we've had our day;
when you see us as dinosaurs,
this, to you, I'd say...
We've worn the latest fashions,
and stayed up, singing all night;
we've danced like demons to music,
and put the world to right.
We know what it is to have a broken heart;
to see the world through tears.
We have all that experience,
which comes with older years.
There's nothing new that you can do,
that we haven't already done.
We've covered just about everything;
everything under the sun.

So! Teenagers, as you grow older,
with teenagers of your own,
when you're wondering what to say,
simply read them this poem!

Once

I was in love, once;
before you knew me.
I was different, then.
My eyes shone brighter, and my heart was aglow;
I looked not on the ways of the world,
for my feet walked lightly,
as on freshly-fallen snow.
I cared, once;
before I became care-less.
I was different, then.
My mind was set on higher thoughts,
and my soul flew, weightless, in the lofty sky.
I sought not the praise of others,
nor the approval of passers-by.
I was me, once,
before the clouds came.
I was different, then.
My passion was intense,
and I danced with the energy of a thousand men.
But that was long ago.
Now, I find contentment in solitude,
and dread the coming of the snow.

The Art of Calm

When practicing the art of Calm,
'tis wise to take deep breaths.
It's a fairly gentle pastime,
with no recorded deaths.
It's awfully beneficial,
and lets the brain relax.
It may take a while to become your style,
if you're stressed out to the max.
Begin by breathing in for four,
and counting out for eight.
Focus on the diaphragm.
Forget the worldly weight.
Empty the mind, 'til all is still;
and hum as you exhale.
If you follow these simple steps,
it's impossible to fail.
Drop your shoulders by your sides,
and let that tension go.
Allow yourself the luxury
of being at one with your flow.
Whenever you're feeling anxious,
and your stomach starts to knot,
practice the art aforementioned,
and Calm will be your lot.

Love Yourself

Love yourself.
Before you hand your heart out
to the next big thing,
and before you give your love carelessly away,
to someone bound to drop it,
give it to yourself.
Don't you deserve it?
After all,
there's only one you.
No-one else sees things
quite the way you do,
or has the same style,
or smile,
or the same gift.
Give yourself a lift.
Stop being hard on yourself.
Be content with who you are.
You are enough.
More than enough.
If people don't like that, tough!
Love your passions.
Love your Life.
Make your search not for husband or wife.
Fall in love with the inner you.

Do the things that your soul wants to,
and kindred spirits will draw near;
of that, be assured, and have no fear.
And love yourself.
Love yourself, my dear.

Speak

Speak to me in words of comfort and of joy, now,
for I have found my Truth, and seek no more.
Hide not your heart from me,
for my thinking is not as in the old days;
overly impassioned,
frantic,
furious,
and filled with the measure of unbridled youth.
It is steeped in the words of wise men and women,
and has been touched by the hand of insight,
gained, these sixty-one summers,
under a burning sun, and a mad, mad moon.
Speak to me only in terms of love, now,
that I may quiet my mind;
for my soul has known darkness, and craves the Light.

The Absence of You

In the absence of you,
I spend my nights
drunk on poetry;
high from the scent
of the ink which bleeds
onto the unsuspecting page,
its innocence blighted
by base thought,
hastily scribbled down.
In the absence of you,
I make dinner for one;
a single, solitary candle,
breathing half-light
onto the cutlery,
dull-glimmered,
around a slate place mat.
In the absence of you,
my world goes on.
I have found beauty in silence,
and comfort in the company
of words.
The sense of peace
which pervades the room
is hard-fought for,
in the absence of you.

Simplicity

In dimm'd light, I write.
I love the night.
The moon watches,
uncritical of my reluctant mind,
as, once again,
I wait in the unhurried hour
for that spark of magic
to ignite.
It is only a matter of time.
I can feel words
welling up inside me,
waiting to pour forth.
They strain at the bit,
knowing the gallop is coming,
and jostle for position.
Great words, small words,
all tumble out,
fighting for prominence.
The first few fall at the fence,
and are trampled underfoot
by the deathless beauty
of simplicity.

Open

I am open,
in the same way that a carelessly ripped
tetra pak is open.
Dear, oh, dear!
What a terrible mess I make,
with my overflowing words,
and my brain with no brake.
My eyes are watchful,
and my soul is awake!
And I am open,
spilling my truth everywhere.

Live Fiercely

Live fiercely,
with every ounce of your being.
Live, with a capital 'L'.
Feed your screaming soul
with whatever it hungers for.
To keep the soul unfed,
is to keep a lion unfed.
It will roar at you,
in your quietest moments,
from the eye of its storm.
Live fiercely.
Sate the soul.
Be inspired.
Be wired to Life...
with a capital 'L'...
all those fears and doubts, expel.
Live, like there's no tomorrow,
because one day, there won't be...

Old Soul

If you're an old soul,
prepare to have your heart broken.
Do not expect to be satisfied
by the transience of temporary fixes,
and the passing of days.
You are not cut out for modern ways,
for you are as old as time itself.
Do not hope to be at ease
with the dealings of this world;
its disposable fripperies,
and its malcontents,
who fail to see beauty in the night sky;
or exchange a hello with passers-by.
Expect to be hungry for love;
for art; for adventure;
for without these things,
the road is long,
and wearisome;
and your journey is far from over.

Listen

Listen to your soul, my friend.
It's trying to tell you something.
No, it's not going to
remind you of your doctor's appointment;
or inform you that you have responsibilities to keep;
or that you have much to do before you sleep.
No.
It wants to tell you to observe your Life,
as it is happening;
and, it begs to be heard.
It wants to know why you ignore it,
yet encumber yourself
with the worries of the world,
which you can do nothing about.
It wants to know
why you never feed it,
or heed it,
yet you let the words of others
become your prison.
Give it ear, my friend,
lest their thoughts become your thoughts.
Listen to your soul, my friend,
for it has your interests at heart

Evensong

Evening,
and the gathering dark
brings a chill to the air.
The birdsong has stilled,
and I am alone with my thoughts.
I could let them wander to times past,
and lose myself in a memory;
or wonder what the future will bring,
and lose myself in anticipation
of who knows what!
Better, then, to content myself
with the present;
and count the blessings herein.
I breathe the night air,
and give thanks for this moment.

Life is Good

Life is good,
if a little painful sometimes.
Pain is good.
It teaches us
that there is balance
in all things.
Balance is good;
though there will be times
when your spinning plates will topple,
and all will come crashing down
around you,
leaving you in tears.
Tears are good.
They are nature's release valve.
Without them, we'd probably implode.
Tears are just emotional rain.
Rain is good.
It waters the earth,
and makes plants and flowers grow,
so that Life continues,
as it should.
Life is good!

In Disguise

Who is in disguise today?
Who would rather have it that way,
and not be able to be read,
by persons either living, or dead?
Who would rather put on shades,
to hide the eyes from men and maids,
who may engage you in conversation,
and fill you with dread and consternation?
Who will avoid all confrontation,
when contact is an aberration?
The you that you are trying to hide,
is buried somewhere deep inside.
I'm sure you'd blossom, if we knew who you were;
but you have to believe in yourself, and care
what happens when you hide your gold,
and away from the world, your gifts withhold.
I'm sure you'd be a shining light,
if being exposed wasn't such a fright!
I wish you courage to lose the disguise,
and be yourself in others' eyes!

A Penny for your Thoughts

A penny for your thoughts, my dear,
is far too low a price.
I'd offer twice as much as that,
and give you some advice.
Never dwell on what is gone.
(I can see it in your eyes).
Don't let yourself be jaded
by the world, and all its lies.
Look inside your heart, my dear,
for you need to love yourself, first,
before you let another's words
your sacred bubble burst.
Never let your light be dimmed,
by cynicism, or doubt.
Be yourself, unashamedly,
and let the true you out.
I wish I could convince you
that beauty lies within.
Don't hide behind your make-up,
someone's heart to win.
A penny for your thoughts, my dear;
or two, if you'd prefer.
Then, your mind would be calm and clear,
and would, much better, fare!

Wisdom

Wisdom is what you get
when your world
falls
away,
and you wonder where
you're going to find the strength
to fight on, another day.
It's found in resolve,
and in learning to cope;
in accepting the unchangeable,
and still having hope.
It's what saves us from tomorrow,
and fortifies today;
it puts perspective on the past,
and keeps the demons at bay.
It is gathered grief,
and an ocean of tears;
a breadth of emotions,
and facing your fears.
One thing's for certain,
when day is done.
Wisdom is not easily won!

It Will Get Easier

It will get easier.
Those long, drawn out days and nights of grief,
when each second takes an hour,
will pass.
Nothing lasts forever...
not even the dull ache in the heart,
which hangs so heavily in the breast;
or the pain which stabs
like a thousand darts,
piercing all sensibilities.
The cacophonous silence
of empty rooms
will become music again;
and unattended moments
won't, by default, fall to sorrow.
But, that's tomorrow.
Today, kid, you have to go through it;
until it feels like your chest will burst.
But, know what?
It will get easier.

A Musical Instrument

A musical instrument is a joy for Life;
a companion, second to none.
It soothes the spirit, and warms the blood,
and bids all woe begone.
It is a light upon the way;
and an outlet for the soul.
Blessings are found in every note,
which falls to the player's control.
Music, the universal tongue,
converses easy, and free.
It draws together kindred hearts,
in synchronicity.
A musical instrument is a joy for Life,
of this, you can be sure.
If all of the world played music,
there'd be no time for war.

Trudging Through Treacle

On days when the going is heavy,
and our boots seem full of lead,
we feel like we're trudging through treacle,
and hope for tomorrow, instead.
But there are untold blessings,
hidden by our pain;
blessings, which, if we only look,
can ease our stress and strain.
We woke up this morning...that's enough,
if we have our health and strength.
Life should be lived for its quality,
regardless of its length.
We have food upon the table,
and clothes upon our backs;
we forget these simple blessings,
lying either side of the tracks.
So, next time we're trudging through treacle,
may we count the blessings therein.
They are armour for the battle,
and the day is ours to win!

The Child Within

It would be a mortal sin,
if we should lose the child within.
Adulthood is a better place,
when wonder is written across the face;
and we seek to view through innocent eyes,
for all too soon, our innocence dies!
If we can keep that wonder alive,
we can do more than just survive!
So next time you look upon the world,
let it be as a boy, or girl.
See the colours in the leaf.
Enjoy your footfall on the ground beneath.
Take the time to look around;
listen to each different sound.
Greet the morn with an open mind,
and leave your cynical thoughts behind!
How can we make it through the day,
if we let the small things get in our way?
Live Life to the full, and follow your whim.
It pacifies the child within!

Spark

There is a spark each has within;
some tend its tiny flame;
They nurture it, and watch it grow,
and celebrate the same.
They follow their passions diligently,
and give no thought to fear.
They shun all negativity
whispered in the ear.
Others never find the spark,
(or never seek to look).
There's always a reason why they haven't the time,
but have every excuse in the book.
Tomorrow, they'll start their journey;
but tomorrow never arrives.
They walk along in the same old rut,
and never Live their Lives.
There is a spark each has within,
to tend, or not, as we will.
Some choose the easy pathway,
others, the daunting hill.
Some follow their higher purpose,
while others drift along;
but those who embark on that journey
sing a different song.
This world is bent on misery;
its works are as dark as night.

It needs more Lights to guide it;
and so, that spark?
Ignite!

The Bard of My Backyard

I am the bard of my backyard;
I praise both tree and flower.
I curse the world, and all its ways -
its desire for money, and power.
I write of love, both present and past;
for both draw strong emotion.
My words pour out to soothe the soul.
Empathy is my potion.
I am the bard of my backyard,
and so I write away;
maybe I'll raise a smile or two,
as I go about my day.
Maybe some wisdom will drip from my pen.
Who knows? It's hard to say!
I don't know what I'm writing about,
'til the writing gets underway!
I am the bard of my backyard;
no subject is omitted.
I wait for inspiration –
then pen to paper is committed.
And all those words inside my head,
jostle for position.
I am the bard of my backyard,
and poetry is my mission.

Stars

So many stars,
and not one bright enough
to light my weary way;
for the hour is late,
and my heavy heart
heaves its tired gait
homeward.
So many dreams,
and not one to save the day.
So many blessings,
hovering,
like butterfly on buddleia,
only a reach away.

The Dentist

We all love a trip to the dentist;
it shows in the smile on the face.
We don't need reminding
of what they'll be finding,
when we go to that fearsome place.
The wisdom teeth need extracting.
No ifs, buts, or maybes about it.
You can scream and shout,
but they're coming out,
no reason, now, to doubt it.
"Take away my wisdom teeth?
I'll be Samson, deprived of his mane!
I'm stupid enough...the procedure looks rough,
and I'm not buying into more pain".
"Don't be a fool" said the man with the tool,
reminiscent of a small shepherd's crook.
"The teeth are impacted; they will be extracted
in accordance with the book.
While you're here, never fear,
I may as well do that filling".
It wasn't long before birdsong
was replaced by the sound of drilling.
Every time I opened my mouth,
I'd an urgent need to cough.
It's a good job I'm not nervous.
I'd have bitten his finger off.

But! Where would be without them?
For their work brings us relief.
So here's to the unsung heroes,
those doctors of the teeth.
Long may they serve to keep our mouths fresh,
and look after our pearly whites!
And when we've no more in our head,
may a denture set suffice!

The Greater Shame

He'd fallen by the wayside,
a bottle in his hand.
Nobody stopped to pick him up,
or tried to understand.
For he was just a drunkard,
without a tale to tell;
and if Elsie down the street is right,
he's going straight to Hell.
He's semi-conscious most every night,
and causes the greatest fuss.
"We can't have that going on around here;
he's clearly not one of us."
And so we cast aspersions,
and judge what we don't understand.
We like to think we're ever so good.
We like to think we're grand.
We're thankful that we're not like him,
because it wouldn't happen to us.
We're far too in control for that;
he obviously needs the buzz.
(Oh, how easy it is to condemn,
from up in our ivory tower!)
"You'd think he'd have some self-respect,
some hidden inner power."
And how in Heaven did he get like that?
Did he wake up one morning and say

"I'll become an alcoholic...
where's my first drink of the day?"
A couple of drinks to calm the stress,
was how it all began...
then a couple more,
and to add to the score,
depression took over the man.
Round and round in circles,
in an ever widening swirl,
booze had crept, like silent death,
and scratched away at his world.
We, obviously, wouldn't let that demon
within our vicinity!
Because we're so level-headed,
aren't we...you and me?

This Road

This road I travel is not without snares,
and pitfalls, to catch me unawares.
There are days when rain muddies up the track,
but, on no account, will I turn back.
Too long have I been plodding on,
from midnight until candle-gone,
to even consider slackening pace,
or adopting a state of temporary grace.
Nothing in Life is given for free;
yet this road demands so much of me.
Onward and upward, I will hike;
for while the iron is hot, that's the best time to strike.
Therefore, be watchful in your way,
for in hidden nooks, opportunities lay.
The window doesn't stay open long,
so if, in your heart, there is a song,
then sing it from your very soul,
and watch the road ahead unfold...

The Sparkly Dust

Some call it the X-Factor;
others, the Sparkly Dust.
Whatever you can't put your finger on;
that's the thing that's a must.
It can't be bought on the internet,
as a last-minute eBay deal;
no more than can a musician
buy that thing called 'feel'.
It'll never be outdated, or ever be outdone.
You can watch a thousand performers,
but there will always be one...
one who stands out from the crowd;
who has the ability to wow;
you have your eyes upon them,
though you don't know why, or how.
They have that certain 'je ne sais quoi'
that sets them apart from the rest;
whenever you see them on a stage,
a fire burns in their breast.
Passion plays behind their eyes,
and seeps from every pore.
The art in them is everything,
which is why we shout for more.
Bless those fantastic creatures,
those denizens of the stage.
Long may they continue to keep us in awe,
and our very souls engage.